Small Dog

Color by Numbers
Coloring Book for Adults

COLOR THERAPY COLORING BOOKS

Copyright © 2018 by Color Therapy Coloring Books

All rights reserved. No part of this publication may be reproduced, distributed, or transmitted in any form or by any means, including photocopying, recoding, or other electronic or mechanical methods, without the prior written permission of the publisher.

Helpful Tips for Coloring

- It's always a great idea to try your colored pencils, markers, and gel pens on the Color Test Page first to ensure you're getting the color you're looking for.

- If you find that your marker or gel pen bleeds on the Color Test Page, put a scrap piece of paper behind the page you are coloring.

- Be sure to keep colored pencils sharp for those detail areas.

- Remember to slow down and take your time— the more you enjoy yourself, the happier you'll be with your drawings.

- Have FUN and color outside the lines...it's ok!

COLOR TEST PAGE

COLOR TEST PAGE

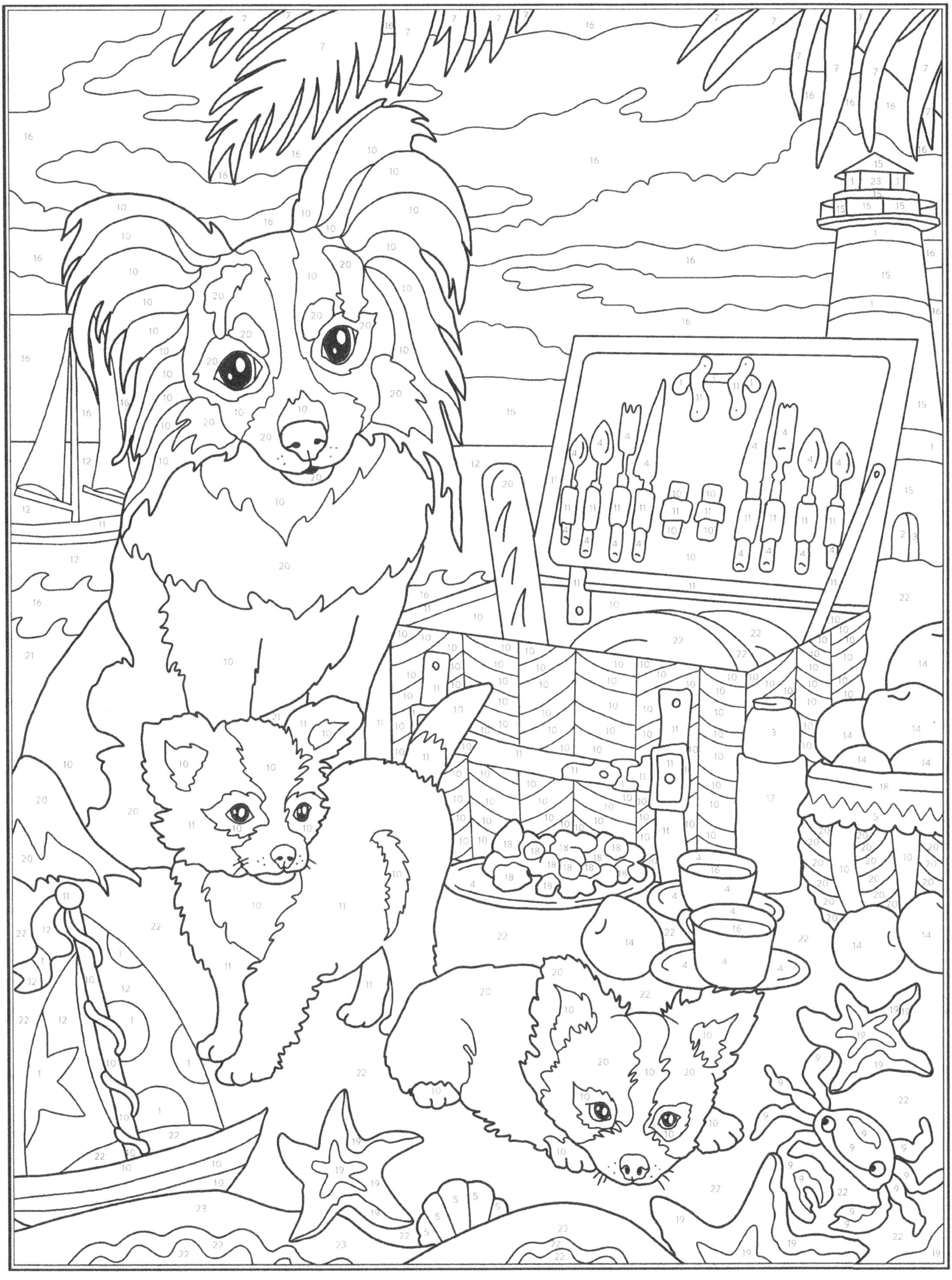

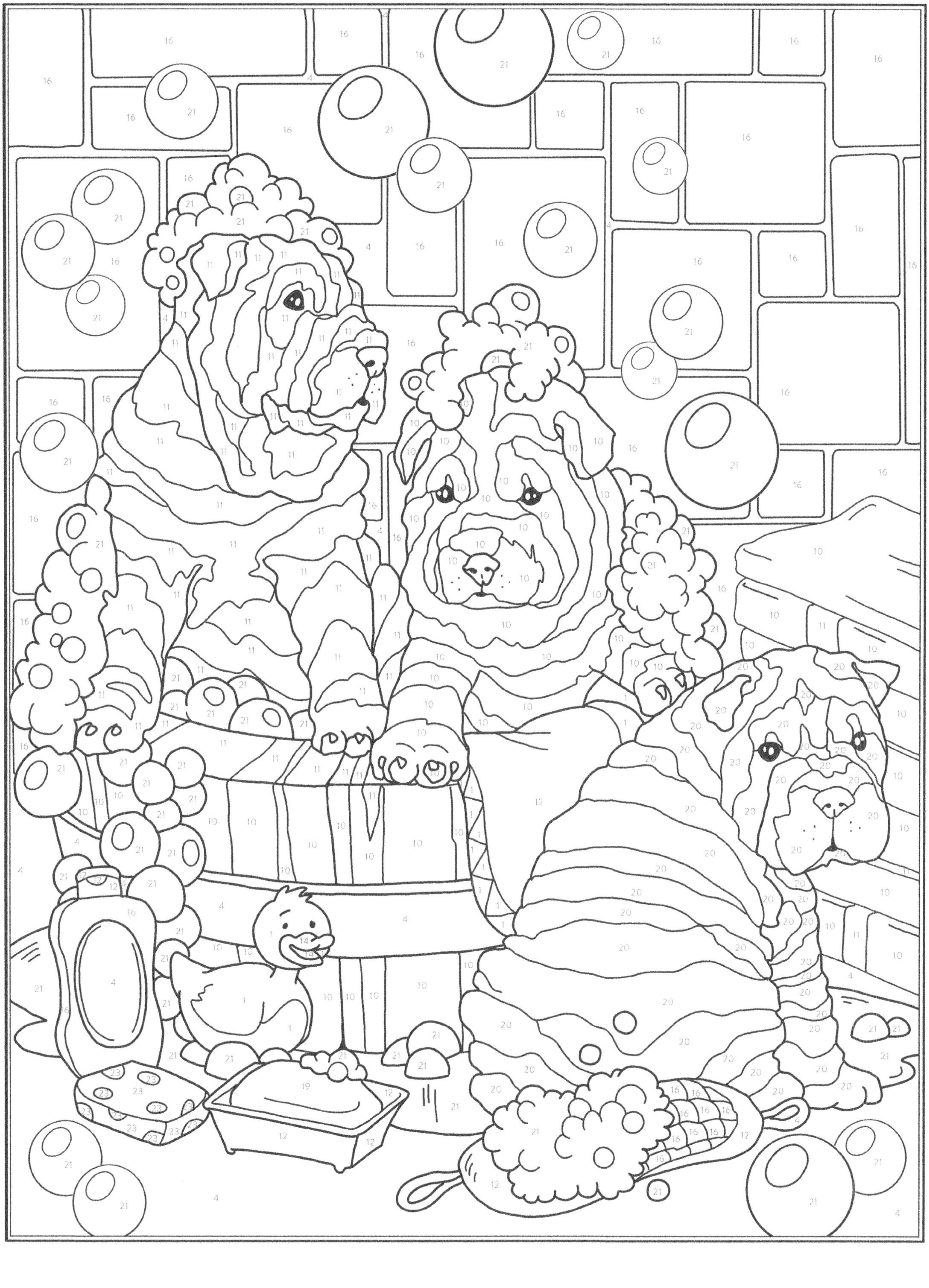

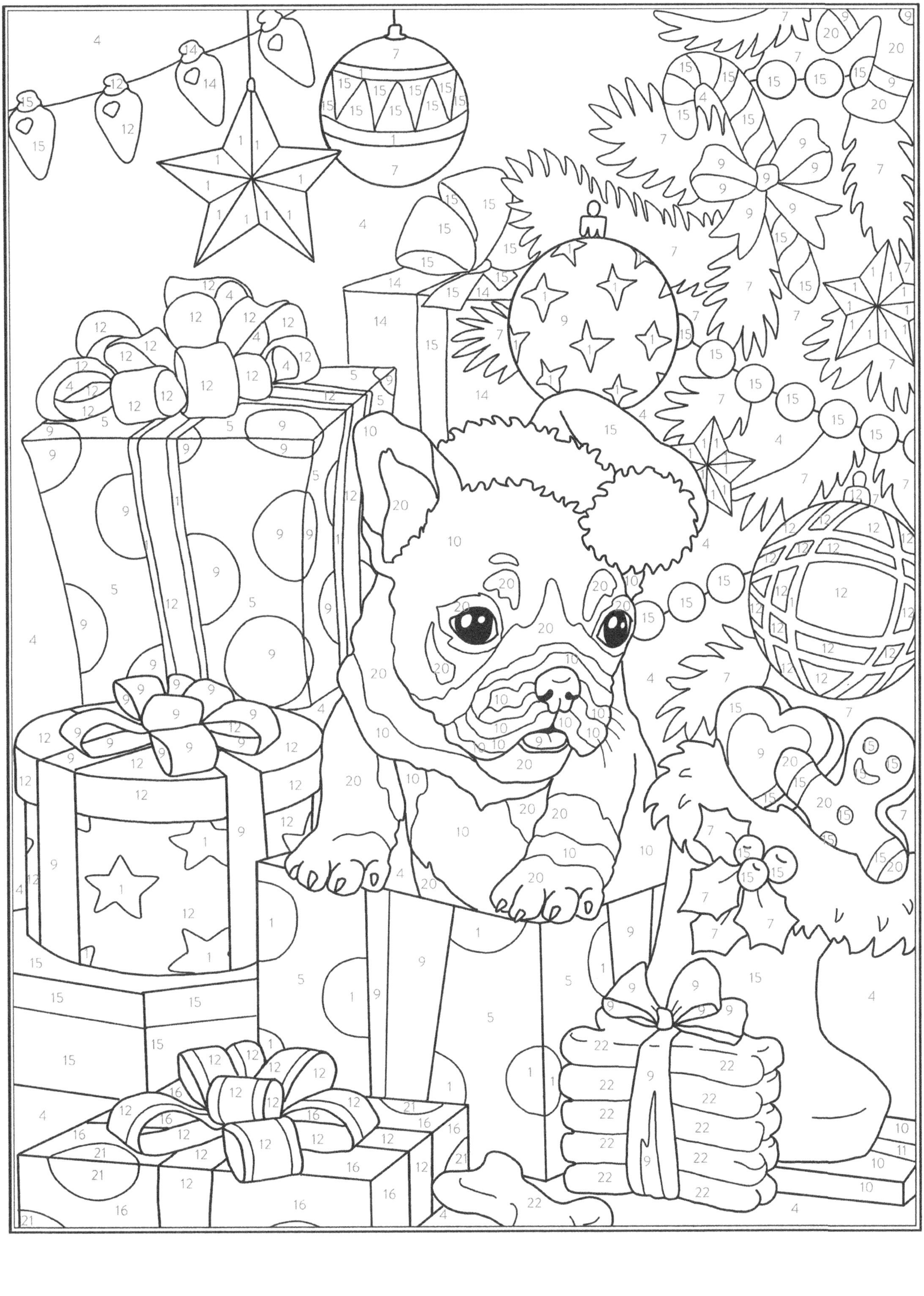

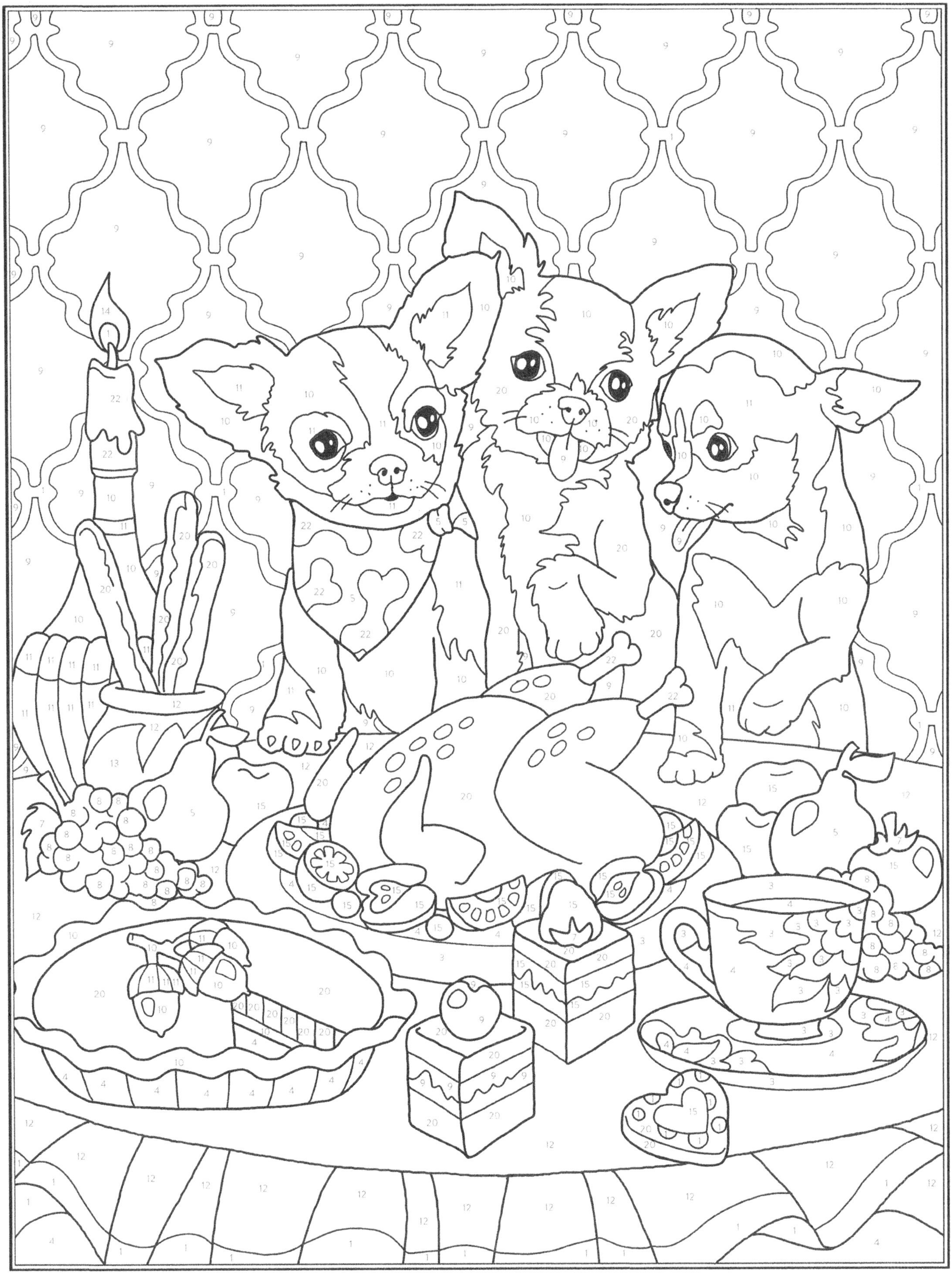

Thank you for choosing

COLOR THERAPY COLORING BOOKS!

We really appreciate your business and would love your feedback! Please share your thoughts on Amazon and add photos of your completed masterpieces!

Made in United States
North Haven, CT
19 March 2023